SCIENTIFIC AMERICAN EDUCATIONAL PUBLISHING

MATH IN ACTION

10 FUN MATH ACTIVITIES

BRING SCIENCE HOME

Published in 2023 by Scientific American Educational Publishing in association with The Rosen Publishing Group
29 East 21st Street, New York, NY 10010

Contains material from Scientific American , a division of Springer Nature America, Inc., reprinted by permission as well as original material from The Rosen Publishing Group.

First Edition

Editor: Jennifer Lombardo
Designer: Rachel Rising

Activity on page 5 by Science Buddies/Ben Finio; page 9 Science Buddies/Svenja Lohner; page 15 by Science Buddies/Ben Finio; page 21 by Science Buddies/Sabine de Brabandere; page 27 Science Buddies/Ben Finio; page 33 Science Buddies/Svenja Lohner; page 39 Science Buddies/Ben Finio; page 43 Science Buddies/Ben Finio; page 49 Science Buddies/Sabine de Brabandere; page 55 Science Buddies/Sabine de Brabandere.

Illustrations by Continuum Content Solutions

Photo Credits: pp. 3,4, 5, 9, 15, 21, 27, 32, 39, 43, 49, 55 cve iv/Shutterstock.com; pp. 4, 5, 9, 15, 21, 27, 33, 39, 43, 49, 55 Anna Frajtova/Shutterstock.com.

Cataloging-in-Publication Data
Names: Scientific American, inc.
Title: Math in action : 10 fun math activities / edited by the Editors of Scientific American.
Description: New York : Scientific American Educational Publishing, 2023. | Series: Bring science home | Includes glossary and index.
Identifiers: ISBN 9781684169634 (pbk.) | ISBN 9781684169641 (library bound) | ISBN 9781684169658 (ebook)
Subjects: LCSH: Mathematics--Juvenile literature. | Mathematics--Experiments--Juvenile literature. | Mathematics--Problems, exercises, etc.--Juvenile literature.
Classification: LCC QA40.5 M384 2023 | DDC 510--dc23

Manufactured in the United States of America

CPSIA Compliance Information: Batch #SACS23. For further information contact Rosen Publishing, New York, New York at 1-800-237-9932.

CONTENTS

THESE ACTIVITIES INCLUDE SCIENCE FAIR PROJECT IDEAS.

INTRODUCTION

Math is more than just addition and subtraction! With the help of math, humans have figured out how to land vehicles on Mars, fight disease, and measure the size of Earth. The projects in this book will help you think more about how math affects our everyday lives, even when we aren't thinking about it.

Projects marked with include a section called Science Fair Project ideas. These ideas can help you develop your own original science fair project. Science fair judges tend to reward creative thought and imagination, and it helps if you are really interested in your project. You will also need to follow the scientific method. See page 61 for more information about that.

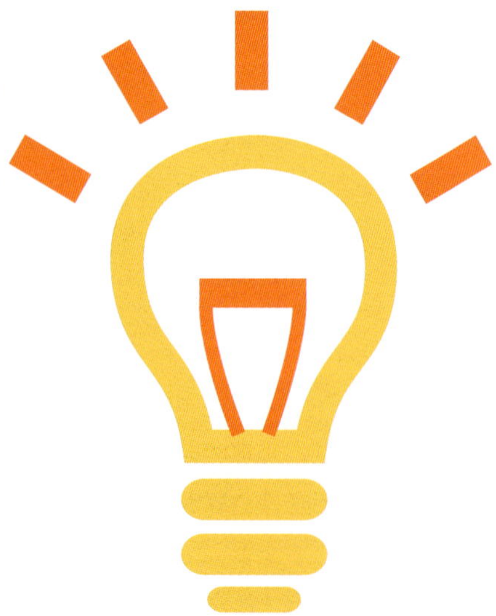

Mars Rover Obstacle Course

EARTH TO MARS: USE PROGRAMMING TO NAVIGATE AROUND ANOTHER ROOM—WITHOUT SETTING FOOT IN IT!

How do scientists and engineers control robots that drive around other planets millions of miles away? It's nowhere near as easy as driving a toy remote-control car here on Earth. In this activity, you will experience some of the challenges you face when driving a "robot" that you can't see!

PROJECT TIME

30 to 45 minutes

KEY CONCEPTS

Mathematics
Physics
Navigation
Programming
Space

BACKGROUND

The U.S. has landed four robotic rovers on Mars: Sojourner in 1997, Spirit and Opportunity in 2004, and Curiosity in 2012. Over the years, these rovers have been given more and more autonomy, meaning they are now able to make some decisions on their own about how to drive around obstacles. They do this by using onboard sensors (such as cameras and lasers) that can detect obstacles and computers to interpret what they see. Scientists on Earth, however, still need to send the rovers commands about where to go. At first you might think this is just like driving a remote-control car, but there's a problem: Mars is very far away from Earth. It's so far away that even the speed of light isn't fast enough for commands to get there without a delay. Depending on where the planets are as they orbit the sun, it can take anywhere between 8 and 20 minutes for a signal to reach Mars from Earth. That means up to 40 minutes round-trip to send a command to the rover and get a response! Can you imagine playing a video game if you had to wait 40 minutes to see what happened every time you pushed a button on the controller?

Because of this delay, when scientists are driving the rover, they need to upload a series of commands all at once to make sure the rover doesn't crash. This requires carefully planning out a path in advance. In this activity, you will work with two volunteers to simulate sending commands between an operator and a rover—and find out some of the challenges and solutions.

MATERIALS

- Two volunteers
- Two adjacent rooms
- Large objects to serve as obstacles, such as furniture or boxes
- Paper and pencil
- Two smartphones or tablets with video chat capabilities (optional)

PREPARATION

- One of your volunteers will be walking around with their eyes closed in this activity. Remove any potentially hazardous obstacles from one of the rooms, such as sharp objects or electrical cords they could trip over.

- Plan a path through this room yourself, from a start location to a finish location. For example, if the room has two doors and a table in the middle, plan how to walk from one door, around the table, and to the other door. Write down exact instructions for following this path. Give each command a number. For example, "1) Take one step forward. 2) Turn right. 3) Take two steps forward. 4) Turn left ...."

- You will be the rover "operator." Assign roles to your two volunteers. One of them will be the "rover," and one will be the "messenger."

PROCEDURE

- Place the rover at the start location in the first room. This person now has to close their eyes and keep them closed. No peeking!

- Go into the other room with the messenger. Make sure you can't see the rover.

- Whisper your first command to the messenger. Make sure you are quiet enough that the rover can't hear you.

- The messenger should now walk (not run) to the other room and tell the command to the rover. The rover should follow the command exactly, but have them be careful to walk very slowly (to avoid any stubbed toes or bumped shins). The messenger should stay in the room with the rover while the rover is moving.

- The messenger should then return to you to get the next command and repeat the process. You aren't allowed to change the commands—stick to what you wrote down!

- Keep sending commands, one at a time, until the rover reaches the finish location or until it "crashes" (for example, by bumping into a piece of furniture or a wall).

- If your rover made it to the finish, congratulations! Now you can switch roles or try adding more obstacles to make the path longer or more complicated. *How complicated can you make the path before your rover crashes?*
- If your rover crashed, don't worry! Talk to your volunteers to try and figure out what went wrong. For example, maybe your steps aren't the same size. In that case, you might need to modify your directions to say, "Take big steps" or "Take small steps," then try again. *How many tries does it take to get your rover from start to finish without crashing?*

SCIENCE FAIR IDEA

If you have two phones or tablets with a video-chat application available, have the rover hold one so you can see what's in front of them (while still keeping their eyes closed). Now you can see what the rover sees. Instead of writing down all your commands in advance, issue them one at a time based on what you see through the video chat. In addition to movement commands, you can also issue commands to control the camera, like "Point the camera down." *Does this make navigating easier or harder?*

OBSERVATIONS AND RESULTS

You might find this activity surprisingly difficult at first! It might be tempting to cheat and modify your commands halfway through, or the rover might want to open their eyes. You might run into problems, such as the rover's steps being bigger or smaller than yours, or the rover not making exactly 90-degree turns. It's important to "calibrate" the rover's motions so you get the results you expect when you issue commands. The same concept applies to the real Mars rovers: To carefully plan a path, scientists need to know exactly how far they will move or turn when they issue a command.

CLEANUP

Put the objects you used as obstacles back where you found them.

What Are the Chances?

HEADS OR TAILS: IS IT A 50-50 CHANCE? CRUNCH SOME NUMBERS AND FLIP SOME COINS TO FIND OUT!

Have you ever heard anyone say the chance of something happening is "50-50"? What does that actually mean? This phrase has something to do with probability. Probability tells you how likely it is that an event will occur. This means that for certain events, you can actually calculate how likely it is that they will happen. In this activity, you will do these calculations and then test them to see whether they hold true for reality!

PROJECT TIME

20 to 30 minutes

KEY CONCEPTS

Mathematics
Probability
Fractions
Percentages

BACKGROUND

Probability allows us to quantify the likelihood an event will occur. You might be familiar with words we use to talk about probability, such as "certain," "likely," "unlikely," "impossible," and so on. You probably also know that the probability of an event happening spans from impossibility, which means that this event will not happen under any circumstance, to certainty, which means that an event will happen without a doubt. In mathematics, these extreme probabilities are expressed as 0 (impossible) and 1 (certain). This means a probability number is always a number from 0 to 1. Probability can also be written as a percentage, which is a number from 0 to 100 percent. The higher the probability number or percentage of an event, the more likely is it that the event will occur.

The probability of a certain event occurring depends on how many possible outcomes the event has. If an event has only one possible outcome, the probability for this outcome is always 1 (or 100 percent). If there is more than one possible outcome, however, this changes. A simple example is the coin toss. If you toss a coin, there are two possible outcomes (heads or tails). As long as the coin was not manipulated, the theoretical probabilities of both outcomes are the same: They are equally probable. The sum of all possible outcomes is always 1 (or 100 percent) because it is certain that one of the possible outcomes will happen. This means that for the coin toss, the theoretical probability of either heads or tails is 0.5 (or 50 percent).

It gets more complicated with a six-sided die. In this case, if you roll the die, there are 6 possible outcomes (1, 2, 3, 4, 5, or 6). Can you figure out what the theoretical probability for each number is? It is 1/6 or 0.17 (or 17 percent). In this activity, you will put your probability calculations to the test. The interesting part about probabilities is that knowing the theoretical likelihood of a certain outcome doesn't necessarily tell you anything about the experimental probabilities when you actually try it out (except when the probability is 0 or 1). For example, outcomes with very low theoretical probabilities do actually occur in reality, although they are very unlikely. So how do your theoretical probabilities match your experimental results? You will find out by tossing a coin and rolling a die in this activity.

MATERIALS

- Coin
- Six-sided die
- Paper
- Pen or pencil

PREPARATION

- Prepare a tally sheet to count how many times the coin has landed on heads or tails.
- Prepare a second tally sheet to count how often you have rolled each number with the die.

PROCEDURE

- Calculate the theoretical probability for a coin to land on heads or tails, respectively. *Write the probabilities in fraction form. What is the theoretical probability for each side?*
- Now get ready to toss your coin. *Out of the 10 tosses, how often do you expect to get heads or tails?*
- Toss the coin 10 times. After each toss, record if you got heads or tails in your tally sheet.
- Count how often you got heads and how often you got tails. Write your results in fraction form. For example, 3 tails out of 10 tosses would be 3/10 or 0.3. (The denominator will always be the number of times you toss the coin, and the numerator will be the outcome you are measuring, such as the number of times the coin lands on tails.) You could also express the same results looking at heads landings for the same 10 tosses. So that would be 7 heads out of 10 tosses: 7/10 or 0.7. *Do your results match your expectations?*
- Do another 10 coin tosses. *Do you expect the same results? Why or why not?*
- Compare your results from the second round with the ones from the first round. *Are they the same? Why or why not?*
- Continue tossing the coin. This time toss it 30 times in a row. Record your results for each toss in your tally sheet. *What results do you expect this time?*

- Look at your results from the 30 coin tosses and convert them into fraction form. *How are they different from your previous results for the 10 coin tosses?*
- Count how many heads and tails you got for your total coin tosses so far, which should be 50. Again, write your results in fraction form (with the number of tosses as the denominator (50) and the result you are tallying as the numerator). *Does your experimental probability match your theoretical probability from the first step?* (An easy way to convert this fraction into a percentage is to multiply the denominator and the numerator each by 2, so 50 x 2 = 100. After you multiply your numerator by 2, you will have a number that is out of 100—and a percentage.)
- Calculate the theoretical probability for rolling each number on a six-sided die. Write the probabilities in fraction form. *What is the theoretical probability for each number?*
- Take the die and roll it 10 times. After each roll, record which number you got in your tally sheet. *Out of the 10 rolls, how often do you expect to get each number?*
- After 10 rolls, compare your results (written in fraction form) with your predictions. *How close are they?*
- Do another 10 rolls with the die, recording the result of each roll. *Do your results change?*
- Now roll the die 30 times in a row (recording the result after each roll). *How often did you roll each number this time?*
- Count how often you rolled each number in all combined 50 rolls. Write your results in fraction form. *Does your experimental probability match your theoretical probability?* (Use the same formula you used for the coin toss, multiplying the denominator and the numerator each by 2 to get the percentage.)
- Compare your calculated probability numbers with your actual data for both activities (coin and die). *What do your combined results tell you about probability?*

SCIENCE FAIR IDEA

Increase the number of coin tosses and die rolls even further. *How do your results compare with the calculated probabilities with increasing number of events (tosses or rolls)?*

SCIENCE FAIR IDEA

Look up how probabilities can be represented by probability trees. *Can you draw a probability tree for the coin toss and die roll?*

SCIENCE FAIR IDEA

If you are interested in more advanced probability calculations, find out how you can calculate the probability of a recurring event. For example: *How likely it is that you would get two heads in a row when tossing a coin?*

OBSERVATIONS AND RESULTS

Calculating the probabilities for tossing a coin is fairly straightforward. A coin toss has only two possible outcomes: heads or tails. Both outcomes are equally likely. This means that the theoretical probability to get either heads or tails is 0.5 (or 50 percent). The probabilities of all possible outcomes should add up to 1 (or 100 percent), which they do. When you tossed the coin 10 times, however, you most likely did not get five heads and five tails. In reality, your results might have been 4 heads and 6 tails (or another non-5-and-5 result). These numbers would be your experimental probabilities. In this example, they are 4 out of 10 (0.4) for heads and 6 out of 10 (0.6) for tails. When you repeated the 10 coin tosses, you probably ended up with a different result in the second round. The same was probably true for the 30 coin tosses. Even when you added up all 50 coin tosses, you most likely did not end up in a perfectly even probability for heads and tails. Your experimental probabilities thus probably didn't match your calculated (theoretical) probabilities.

You likely observed a similar phenomenon when rolling the die. Although the theoretical probability for each number is 1 out of 6 (1/6 or 0.17), in reality your experimental probabilities probably looked different. Instead of rolling each number 17 percent out of your total rolls, you might have rolled them more or less often.

If you continued tossing the coin or rolling the die, you probably have observed that the more trials (coin tosses or die rolls) you did, the closer the experimental probability was to the theoretical probability. Overall, these results mean that even if you know the theoretical probabilities for each possible outcome, you can never know what the actual experimental probabilities will be if there is more than one outcome for an event. After all, a theoretical probability is just predicting how the chances are that an event or a specific outcome occurs—it won't tell you what will actually happen!

CLEANUP

Put the die and coins back where you found them.

Science with a Smartphone

Measure Light with Lux

HOW DARK IS THE NIGHT? USE A SMARTPHONE OR TABLET TO FIND OUT AND LEARN ABOUT MEASURING LIGHT.

Did you know you can use a smartphone as a scientific instrument to explore the world around you? Smartphones contain many built-in electronic sensors that can measure phenomena such as sound, light, motion and more. In this activity, you'll use the light sensor on a phone or a tablet to examine the brightness of light from different light sources and locations. How bright is the reading lamp in your living room compared with direct sunlight? Try this activity to find out!

PROJECT TIME

20 to 30 minutes

KEY CONCEPTS

Physics
Light
Measurement
Mathematics

BACKGROUND

Measuring things around you, such as distance, is probably pretty familiar. Units of measurement, such as inches or centimeters, can describe the distance between one point and another. However, there are many other qualities in the world around us that we can also turn into measurable quantities. For example, did you know you can measure light? You might describe light levels relative to other things, such as "dark as night" or "brighter than the sun," but you probably wouldn't use a number. However, just as you might need a ruler to measure a distance, you can use a tool to measure precise units of light.

Light can be measured in different ways. One unit of measurement is called a lux, which describes how much light falls on a certain area. (This is different from a unit of lumens, which tells you the total amount of light emitted by a light source.) The number of lux gets smaller as you get farther away from a light source. This makes sense if you think about it: A light bulb looks much dimmer if you are standing 100 feet (30.5 m) away from it instead of up close—even though it is still emitting the same total amount of light in lumens. Typical outdoor lux levels can range from less than 1/1,000 lux on a dark night to more than 30,000 lux in direct sunlight!

This is where a smartphone comes in handy. There have long been stand-alone lux meters (for use in photography, for example)—devices with a light sensor and a screen that would display light levels in lux units. Current smartphones and tablets, however, generally contain built-in light sensors that are used to automatically adjust screen brightness based on light levels (for example, making the screen brighter and easier to see if you're using the device in direct sunlight but dimming the screen in darker environments so it's not too bright for your eyes). Many phones can run apps that will display the light reading in lux units. To learn more about light levels in the world around you, find a smartphone or tablet and start measuring!

MATERIALS

- Smartphone or tablet with internet access and permission to download and install an app
- Adult (to help verify and download the app)
- Different light sources (flashlight, lamp, ceiling light, etc.)
- Different locations (dark closet, room with windows, outdoors, etc.)
- Ruler (optional)

PREPARATION

- Ask an adult to help you search for a "lux meter" or "light meter" app on a smartphone or tablet. There are many free options available (note that some apps might have ads or in-app purchases enabled).

- Get to know your lux meter app. Some apps will just display a number on the screen, whereas others will display a meter or a graph. Some will also let you record data. Make sure the app is working; move your phone from a dark room to a bright room or hold it close to a light bulb (bulbs are also hot as well as bright, so be careful here), and you should see the numbers fluctuate.

- Locate the light sensor on your device. It is usually near the top on the front of the phone (the side with the screen). You can do this by running your fingertip over the surface of the phone while your lux meter app is open. When your finger covers the light sensor the reading should drop. Make sure you do not accidentally cover the sensor while doing the activity.

- Note: Some apps might display light levels in other units, such as "EV," which stands for "exposure value" and is used in photography to measure the amount of light hitting a camera. The concepts explained in this activity still apply, and you can still compare different light sources or how light levels change with distance from a light source. The numbers you measure in EV, however, will not be the same that you would measure in lux.

PROCEDURE

- Test how lux readings change with distance from a fixed light source. For example, stand directly under a ceiling light, hold your phone with the screen facing up, and move the phone up and down. Alternatively, hold the phone sideways and aim it toward a floor lamp as you walk closer to and farther away from the lamp. *How do the readings change with distance?*

- Now compare different artificial light sources at the same distance. You can use a ruler for this or any convenient object (or a body part, such as your forearm) as a spacer. *The exact distance doesn't matter as long as you keep it constant. How does a flashlight compare with a light bulb? What about the light from a TV or computer screen? What light source in your house is the brightest? The dimmest?*
- Finally, measure ambient light levels in different locations. Turn off all sources of artificial light. *How do light levels outside compare with light levels inside? What about in a room with window coverings closed versus the window coverings open? In the room where you sleep at night versus during the day? Which room in your house gets the most natural light? Which room gets the least?*

SCIENCE FAIR IDEA

Try tilting your phone relative to a light source and watch how the readings change.

OBSERVATIONS AND RESULTS

You probably noticed how dramatically lux change with distance from a light source. You might only read a few tens or hundreds of lux when you are across the room from a light bulb, but if you hold your phone right up to the bulb, the reading could be in the thousands or even tens of thousands. This is because of a mathematical relationship called the inverse square law. As the light expands outward from the source, the amount of light hitting each area drops off very rapidly. The sun is so far away you might find it surprising that lux readings in direct sunlight are so high (in the tens of thousands of lux). This gives us a sense of just how very bright the sun itself is!

If you tried tilting your phone, you might have noticed that the readings decreased—even though your phone's distance from the light source didn't change. The angle of a surface relative to the light source also determines how much light hits it because light travels in a straight line. A surface that is perpendicular (at a 90-degree angle) to the light rays will collect the most light. This is why it's important for solar panels to be aimed directly at the sun—and why Earth's poles get less light (and are colder) than the equator.

Having a unit of measurement and a device to measure it can be useful for determining and comparing different environments more specifically. You might find, for example, that a specific range of lux is the most comfortable for you to read a book. These measurements can be used for designing buildings, such as schools, to ensure there is the right amount of light for different areas and activities.

Depending on your phone or the app you used, the range of values you were able to measure might have been limited. Some apps, for example, might not display decimal readings, making it difficult to measure light levels below 1 lux (in other words, even if the real reading is 0.4 lux, the app would display 0 lux). This would be most common in very dark locations, such as inside a closet or outside at night. The maximum reading could also be limited by the app or the phone's or tablet's hardware. You might, for example, only see a reading of 10,000 lux outside in direct sunlight—even if you expected a reading of 30,000 lux or more. This is useful to remember when using any measuring device. Just as the length of a ruler can't reflect the full length of a soccer field—or a kitchen thermometer couldn't tell us the temperature of the sun's surface—many digital measuring tools aren't able to provide a complete range of possible measurements.

CLEANUP

Put any light sources you may have moved back where you found them.

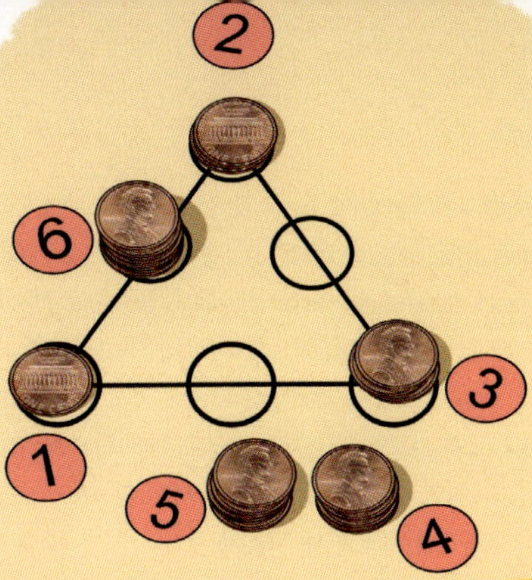

Math Fun with a Perimeter Magic Triangle

COUNT YOUR PENNIES! LEARN A FUN PUZZLE TO TEST YOUR QUICK COMPUTATION SKILLS—AND SEE IF YOU CAN FIND NEW STRATEGIES FOR GETTING SPEEDY SOLUTIONS.

Do you ever use math as a tool to solve interesting problems? In the 1970s, math was often taught with simple worksheets. One teacher was looking for a way to help his students have more fun with math and logic. So he developed what is now known as the perimeter magic triangle puzzles. Try them out—and have some fun as you start thinking about counting in a whole new way!

PROJECT TIME

45 to 60 minutes

KEY CONCEPTS

Mathematics
Addition
Counting
Puzzles

BACKGROUND

Counting is so common that we forget how it is connected to the broader area of mathematics that studies numbers, known as arithmetic. We can see counting as repeatedly adding one: when you add one object to another you have two objects. Add one more and you have three, and so on. Addition is the process of adding numbers. The result of the addition is called the sum. With smaller numbers, you might use counting to find the sum. When you have three and want to add two, for example, you can count two numbers beyond three to get to five. With plenty of practice, you can often memorize the sums of the numbers 1 through 10—at which point it can be fun to play with numbers to find all the ways you can make a particular sum.

Math puzzles and games can be a fun way to get practice working with numbers. Puzzles also provide entertaining ways to build strategic and logical thinking. With a little trial and error, you can often start to find new strategies to complete a puzzle faster. These are the very same techniques mathematicians use: starting small and trying to find patterns in the sequence of answers. These patterns are then used to predict the answers to even bigger puzzles.

If this is all too abstract, try the puzzle presented in this activity! It might make the process of learning arithmetic clear.

MATERIALS

- Two sheets of 9-by-12-inch (23 by 30 cm) paper, such as construction or craft paper (if possible, choose contrasting colors)
- Pencil or marker
- Ruler
- Scissors
- A quarter or other round object of similar size
- 21 pennies, small blocks, or other small stackable objects
- More sheets of paper (optional)

PREPARATION

- Draw a large triangle on a sheet of paper (you can use a ruler to help make straight lines).

- Use a quarter to trace a circle on each corner of the triangle. Now trace a circle onto the middle of each side of the triangle. You should have six circles.
- On the bottom of the second sheet of paper, draw six circles similar in size to the ones drawn on the triangle.
- Cut out these circles and number them 1 through 6. These circles will be referred to as number disks.
- Keep the top part of the second sheet of paper. You will use it to write down your results.

PROCEDURE

- On the paper with the triangle, use the 21 pennies to build towers on each circle. Each circle must have at least one penny, but no two towers can be of the same height. Can you do it?
- Keep trying until you find a solution!
- Count the number of pennies in each tower. Write down each sum in order from the smallest to the largest number. What do you notice about this set of numbers?
- Shift the towers around or rebuild them until you can fulfill one more requirement: The total number of pennies used to build the three towers on each side of the triangle must be the same. If you build towers of 1, 5, and 3 pennies in the circles lining up on one side of the triangle, for example, you used 1 + 5 + 3 = 9 pennies on that side. Lining up towers of 1, 2, and 4 pennies on the adjacent side would not work because 1+ 2 + 4 = 7—not 9 like the first side. (Notice the tower of 1 penny was placed on the corner of this triangle, so it contributes to two sides.) If you tried 1, 2, and 6 for the adjacent side instead, that works because 1 + 2 + 6 = 9. Now you can place the one tower that is left and check if 9 pennies are used in the three towers on the third side of this triangle. Try it out! Did you find a solution?

- If this is not a solution, think. *Can you rearrange a few towers and get a solution?*
- If working with abstract numbers is easier for you, replace the towers with the number disks. Each number disk then represents a tower of pennies. The number written on the number disks informs you of the number of pennies in that tower.
- Using nine pennies per side is possible! *Did you find the solution? Are there several ways you can arrange the towers so there are nine pennies used per side?*
- *Can you arrange the pennies so you use 10, 11, or even 12 pennies per side?*

SCIENCE FAIR IDEA

The puzzle presented in this activity is called a "perimeter magic triangle of order three." To extend it to a higher-order perimeter magic triangle, start by drawing a new triangle. Add circles on the corners like you did the first time, but this time, add two more circles on each side in between the corners. For this puzzle, you will need nine number disks. Number them 1 through 9. Just like in the previous puzzle, you need to find ways to place the disks on the circles so the sums of the numbers on each side of this triangle are identical. Mathematicians call this triangle a triangle of order four because it has four numbers on each side. Once you have solved this puzzle, continue with a triangle of order five (add three more circles between the corners and cut 12 number disks), then order six, and so on.

SCIENCE FAIR IDEA

Can you create a strategy to find solutions for this type of puzzle quickly?

SCIENCE FAIR IDEA

Show that there are no solutions that use eight or fewer pennies per side—or show that there are no solutions with a total of 13 or more pennies per side.

OBSERVATIONS AND RESULTS

Did you find that you can only arrange the 21 pennies in towers of 1, 2, 3, 4, 5, and 6 pennies if you need to make 6 towers of different heights? Could you come up with ways to arrange the towers so the sum of pennies used on each side of the triangle is identical for all 3 sides? It is possible for a total of 9, 10, 11, and 12 pennies per side.

To use a total of 9 pennies on each side, you place the towers with 1, 2, and 3 pennies on the corners of the triangle. The tower of 6 pennies goes in between the towers of 1 and 2 pennies because 1 + 2 + 6 = 9. The tower of 5 pennies stands between the tower of 1 and the tower of 3 pennies, as 1 + 3 + 5 also equals 9. The towers with 2, 4, and 3 pennies fill up the third row. Notice how the smallest towers are placed on the corners for this solution.

To arrange the towers so that you use 12 pennies on each side, start by arranging the tallest towers (those with 6, 5, and 4 pennies) on the corners of your triangle and fill in the circles in between. Place the smallest tower you have left (1 penny tall) in between the 2 tallest towers (5 and 6 pennies each). Do you see that the smallest one you are left with (2 pennies tall) goes in between the tallest ones that need a tower in between (the towers with 6 and 4 pennies each)?

A strategy you could use to find the solution that has 10 pennies on each side is listing all the ways you can make 10 by adding 3 different numbers. You will find 3 + 2 + 5 = 10, 5 + 4 + 1 = 10, and 1 + 6 + 3 = 10. Can you see that 3, 5, and 1 are part of 2 of these sums? This means these go on the corners of your triangle. You can use the same strategy to find out how to place the pennies so there are 11 or 12 pennies used on each side.

Are you wondering how you can know that using 8 pennies per side is not possible? With 8 pennies per side, you use 3 X 8, or 24, pennies for the triangle. Because you reuse the pennies on the corner towers you at most use 1 + 2 + 3 (the sum of the 3 smallest towers), or 6 pennies fewer. In other words, you can use at most 18 pennies. The puzzle asks you to use 21.

CLEANUP

Put away the pennies you used.

Lift Water with an Archimedes Screw

LEARN HOW THE ANCIENT GREEKS PUMPED WATER UPHILL—WITH AN INNOVATIVE TWIST ON BASIC PHYSICS!

Can you think of a way to make water run uphill—without using electricity? The ancient Greeks discovered how to do just this! They developed a device called the Archimedes screw to lift water from one location to another. This tool is so useful that it is still in widespread use today. In this activity, you will build your own hand-powered Archimedes screw from simple materials.

PROJECT TIME

60 to 75 minutes

KEY CONCEPTS

Physics
Liquids
Geometry
Engineering

BACKGROUND

Archimedes of Syracuse was born in the 3rd century B.C. He liked to solve problems and was one of the most important inventors of his time. The king requested that Archimedes build the biggest ship possible. This ship proved to be leaky, and Archimedes had to invent a device to remove water from it. So he designed what we now call the Archimedes screw. It was very effective because it got rid of the water and only required one person to operate it. The Archimedes screw was soon also used to transport water from low-lying areas up to irrigation ditches. The design is so effective that it is still being used today. For instance, it is used to lift wastewater in water treatment plants and even to lift water in some amusement park rides. It's a tool that has never gone out of style.

The Archimedes screw is a form of positive-displacement pump. A positive-displacement pump traps fluid from a source and then forces the fluid to move to a discharge location. The Archimedes screw is made up of a hollow cylinder and a spiral part (the spiral can be inside, but here you'll put it outside the cylinder). One end is placed in a low-lying fluid source and the other end is tilted up into a higher discharge area. To move water, all you need to do is rotate the screw. As the screw moves, it scoops up a small amount of water into the first pocket. On the next turn of the screw, the first pocket of water moves to the second pocket, and a new scoop of water enters the first pocket. This motion continues, and eventually the first scoop of water comes out at the other end.

There are many factors that determine how well the Archimedes screw will work, such as the length, its angle, the radius, and more. In this project, you will build and demonstrate your own Archimedes screw. Optionally, you can even try changing the screw design to find out how to make it lift water faster!

MATERIALS

- PVC pipe at least 1 inch (2.5 cm) in diameter and at least 1 foot (30 cm) long
- Clear vinyl tubing at least 1/4 inch diameter (0.6 cm) and at least 2 feet (61 cm) long (these materials can be found at many hardware stores)
- Duct tape
- Scissors
- Two containers for water
- Two items to elevate one of the containers, such as small boxes or additional containers
- A workspace that can tolerate spills

- An adult helper
- Cloth towel for cleaning up spills (optional)
- Food coloring (optional)
- Different diameters and lengths of PVC pipe (optional)
- Different diameters of vinyl tubing (optional)

PREPARATION

- Attach one end of the vinyl tubing to one end of the PVC pipe with duct tape. Ensure that the opening to the tubing is open (not blocked by the tape).
- Tightly wrap the tubing around the pipe in a spiral.
- Attach the tubing to the other end of the pipe with duct tape, again being careful to not block the opening of the tubing.
- Have an adult help use scissors to cut off any extra tubing.
- If necessary, use extra pieces of duct tape to evenly space out the tubing along the length of the pipe.

PROCEDURE

- Fill one of your containers with water. Optionally, you can add food coloring to make the water easier to see when it is in the tubing.
- Elevate the second (empty) container so it is higher than the first container.

- Place one end of your Archimedes screw in the lower container of water, and align the other end over the upper container.
- Rotate the screw so the bottom end of the tubing "scoops" water with each rotation. It should go underwater and then come back above the surface with each revolution and not remain completely submerged the entire time. If you do not see your tubing start to fill with water after a few rotations, you might be spinning the screw the wrong direction. *When you look at your screw from the side, what do you see? How is the water distributed in the tubing?*
- Keep rotating the screw, and watch as the water moves up into the higher container!
- Try different ways of using your Archimedes screw. *How high can you lift water?* Raise the upper container, and tilt the screw upward at a steeper angle. *Do you reach a point where water starts to flow back down the tube instead of up?*

SCIENCE FAIR IDEA

Try different designs of your Archimedes screw. *What happens if you change the spacing of the tubing spiral, making the individual turns closer together or farther apart? What if you change the diameter of the PVC pipe or the tubing?*

OBSERVATIONS AND RESULTS

How does the Archimedes screw manage to move water uphill? When you bend the tubing into a spiral shape, it forms individual pockets where water can get trapped because the tubing curves upward on both sides. If you look at your screw from the side, you will see these pockets filled with water. As you rotate the screw, it traps alternating pockets of air and water, and the individual pockets move up the screw to the upper container. If you tilt the screw up at too steep of an angle, eventually one side of each pocket will point downhill, allowing the water to flow back down. This is easiest to see if you stand the pipe up vertically—notice how there is nowhere for the water to get "trapped" without flowing downhill.

CLEANUP

Wipe up any water that may have spilled.

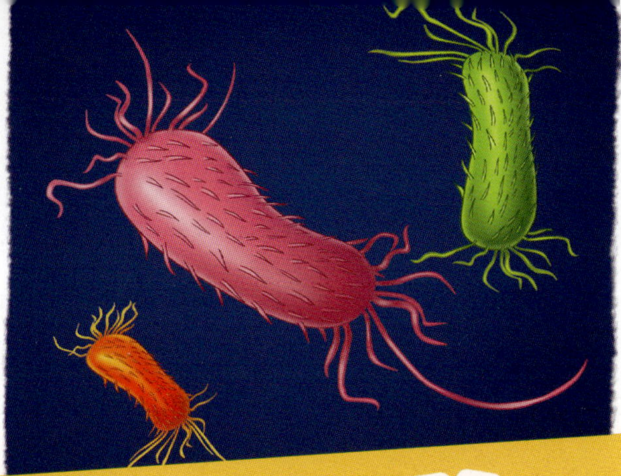

How Do You Stop Superbugs?

WHAT'S BUGGING YOU? LEARN HOW MEDICINE WORKS BEST TO FIGHT COMMON BACTERIA!

Have you ever had to take antibiotics? Your doctor or nurse probably told you to finish taking every dose of the medication—even if you start to feel better before you finish it. Why is that? You might be surprised to learn that if you stop taking antibiotics early, you might contribute to the creation of antibiotic-resistant "superbugs," which can make our medicine less effective—and illnesses harder to treat. In this activity, you will find out why these superbugs are so difficult to treat by rolling dice to see how bacteria respond to antibiotics.

PROJECT TIME

30 to 45 minutes

KEY CONCEPTS

Biology
Bacteria
Health
Medicine
Mathematics
Probability

BACKGROUND

Bacteria are microscopic organisms that are everywhere. Even when we are healthy, trillions of them live on and in our bodies. Most bacteria are harmless to humans—and many are beneficial. However, some can make us sick. Antibiotics are drugs that treat bacterial infections, such as strep throat or ear infections, by killing bacteria. Before antibiotics became widely used in the mid-20th century, people sometimes died from minor wounds and infections (perhaps injuries we might think of as trivial, such as a scraped knee).

Over time, however, many antibiotics have lost their effectiveness because bacteria have become more resistant to them. This means some bacteria can survive the antibiotics that were supposed to kill them. These bacteria are known as antibiotic-resistant bacteria, or "superbugs."

This happens because not all bacteria are the same: Some bacteria can be more resistant to an antibiotic than others. If some bacteria are not as susceptible to the antibiotic, they can survive—and even multiply.

Scientists agree that taking antibiotics for too short of a time increases the risk of creating antibiotic resistance in surviving bacteria. Other actions that can lead to antibiotic-resistant bacteria are taking antibiotics when they aren't necessary (such as when you are sick with a virus), not disposing of antibiotics properly, or taking antibiotics for too long. In this activity, you will model the development of antibiotic-resistant bacteria with dice. How many doses do you think it will take to wipe out all of them?

MATERIALS

- 20 dice (6-sided: 15 of one color and 5 of another color) or access to an online dice roller or offline dice roller app
- Paper
- Pen
- Large, flat work area where you can roll all the dice (if you are using physical dice)
- Additional dice of each color (optional)
- Graphing paper (optional)

PREPARATION

- Divide the dice by color. In your model, each die will represent one bacterium, with the five dice of the same color representing the more-resistant bacteria and the 15 dice of the other color representing the less-resistant bacteria. (In nature, luckily, the less-resistant bacteria are still the most abundant.)

- Write on your paper which color represents which bacteria.

- In your simulation, each roll of the dice will correspond to taking one dose of antibiotics. The more-resistant bacteria will survive the antibiotics when their roll is a 2, 3, 4, 5, or 6. Less-resistant bacteria only survive when their roll is a 6. *How are the survival probabilities different for the less-resistant versus the more-resistant bacteria?*

PROCEDURE

- Mix all your dice together and roll them to represent the first dose of antibiotics.

- Separate the rolled dice into a "surviving" pile and a "died" pile based on the rules for the less-resistant and more-resistant bacteria. *How did the first dose of antibiotics do in killing off bacteria?*

- Set all the dice in the "died" pile aside. They will not be used anymore. Count how many dice of each color are in the "surviving" pile, and record your results on a piece of paper. *How many bacteria survived? How many of the more-resistant or less-resistant bacteria died?*

- Repeat these steps until no dice are left. Record your results every time you roll the dice. *How many rolls does it take to kill all of the more-resistant bacteria? Do the more-resistant bacteria survive longer or for less time compared with the less-resistant ones? Why do you think this is the case?*

SCIENCE FAIR IDEA

Increase the number of dice for each bacteria group or change the ratio of more-resistant versus less-resistant bacteria. *How does this change your results? What happens if you start out with a larger proportion of more-resistant bacteria?*

SCIENCE FAIR IDEA

Use graphing paper to graph your results. On the horizontal axis, write the number of doses (how many times you roll the dice), and on the vertical axis, graph the number of survived bacteria after each dose. *How do your graphs for the more-resistant versus less-resistant bacteria compare?*

SCIENCE FAIR IDEA

In the real world, live bacteria can multiply, creating more of their own type of bacterium. *What do you think will happen if you allow each bacterium to multiply over time?* Go through two doses of antibiotics (rolls of the dice), removing the "dead" bacteria each time. After the second dose, remove the "dead" bacteria as usual, but this time add in a die of the same color for each bacterium that survived. *What did that do to the ratio of more-resistant and less-resistant bacteria?* Continue to do this after every two rolls of the dice. *What happens to the ratio of bacteria? Are you able to wipe out the more-resistant bacteria eventually? Can you think about why it is important to avoid the presence of more-resistant bacteria in the first place?*

SCIENCE FAIR IDEA

Antibiotics only work to kill off bacteria. *What happens if you have a virus, which is caused by a different type of infection, such as the common cold?* Let's find out. Gather the 15 dice of the same color; this time these will be the virus cells. Now roll all of the dice, representing one dose of antibiotics. *Remove any die that landed on a 7. Did the antibiotic kill any of the virus cells?*

OBSERVATIONS AND RESULTS

Were you able to kill all the bacteria? Probably yes, but it might have taken you many rounds of rolling the dice to do so. You probably noticed that the "normal," or less-resistant, bacteria got killed off pretty quickly. They only survived in your model when the roll outcome was a six, and with six possible numbers on the die, the probability for them surviving one roll (representing one dose of antibiotics) was only one out of six, which is 16.6 percent. It likely took only a few rolls to eliminate all less-resistant bacteria.

The more-resistant bacteria in this model, however, have a survival probability of five out of six, or 83.3 percent for each roll (or dose), as they survive when a two, three, four, five, or six is rolled. This means that it should have taken much longer to kill all the more-resistant bacteria. Even though they start out at a much lower number than the less-resistant bacteria, after a few rolls they were probably the only ones alive. It might have taken you up to 10—or even more—doses of antibiotics (or dice rolls) to wipe out all of them.

This is what happens in real life with bacteria. One dose of antibiotics is very efficient in killing off a lot of bacteria that can't resist the effects of the drug. Bacteria that can defend themselves against the antibiotics, however, are able to survive the first dose, and it will take several doses of treatment to kill them. If you tried the additional activity of allowing the surviving bacteria to multiply, you probably saw that it was extremely difficult to kill off the more-resistant bacteria. This is why we try to avoid having more of these bugs in the first place. And if you tried to kill off viruses with antibiotic doses, you of course saw that it didn't work at all! So keep this in mind for the next time you are sick. Take any prescribed antibiotics exactly as your doctor or nurse instructs—so you can do your part and help avoid the creation of superbugs.

CLEANUP

If you used physical dice, put them away.

Build Your Own Mini-Golf Course

CAN YOU MASTER THE MINI-GOLF COURSE? A LITTLE PHYSICS CAN GO A LONG WAY IN HELPING YOU TO SINK A HOLE IN ONE!

Have you ever played mini-golf? It might seem like just a fun game, but there's a lot of science behind it! Learn about the physics behind a rolling, bouncing mini-golf ball—and design your own mini-golf course in this fun science activity.

PROJECT TIME

60 to 75 minutes

KEY CONCEPTS

Physics
Angles
Energy
Friction

BACKGROUND

In most mini-golf courses, there is not a direct path from where you start the ball to the hole. You often have to get the ball around, over, or under one or more obstacles. Your goal is to get the ball into the hole by hitting it as few times as possible—which can be difficult with all that stuff in the way. One way to accomplish this is to bounce the ball off walls or other obstacles. By carefully planning out the ball's path, you could even get a hole in one!

If you watch the ball carefully when it hits a wall, you will probably notice that the angle at which the ball hits the wall (known as the angle of incidence) is nearly identical to the angle at which the ball bounces back off of the wall (known as the angle of reflection). There might be a slight change due to the ball's spin, but if you bounce the ball off a wall at a certain angle, it should rebound at roughly the same angle. This allows you to get the ball around obstacles. You will also notice that eventually your ball slows down and stops. The kinetic energy of the ball as it rolls is gradually converted to heat due to friction with the ground.

Now that you know a little more about the physics behind mini-golf, you're prepared to design your own holes—complete with fun obstacles!

MATERIALS

- Paper
- Scissors
- Pencil
- Ruler
- Tape
- Large table or counter
- Small rubber bouncy ball
- Assorted sturdy, small-but-heavy household items, such as cans of food, a metal stapler, a roll of duct tape, and so on. The objects should be heavy enough that the ball can bounce off them without moving them.
- Larger ball, such as a tennis ball (optional)
- Larger sturdy objects (optional)

PREPARATION

- Cut two circles out of paper. Label one "start" and one "finish." The smaller you make the "finish" circle, the more difficult the game will be.

PROCEDURE

- Make a few sketches of different mini-golf hole designs before you start building. Draw the start location, finish location, and any obstacles you want to put in between them. Try to include at least one obstacle that blocks the direct path from start to finish.
- *Using what you learned about angles of incidence and reflection in the background section, is it still possible to get a hole in one in your design by bouncing the ball off obstacles or walls?* Use the ruler to draw a series of straight lines representing the ball's path from start to finish. *How many times does the ball have to bounce to make it to the finish location?*
- Now build one of your mini-golf holes by assembling the obstacles and start/finish circles, and try it out! Put the ball on the start circle, and roll it or flick it with your finger. *Can you get a hole in one by following the path you drew on paper?*
- If you don't get a hole in one, keep rolling the ball until you get it to the "finish" spot. Then go back to the start and try again. *Can you get a hole in one if you keep practicing? How closely does the actual path match your predicted path?*
- Repeat the process for some of your other designs. *Are some of them easier than others?*

SCIENCE FAIR IDEA

Instead of rolling the ball with your hand, build your own golf club.

OBSERVATIONS AND RESULTS

You might have found that getting a hole in one was more difficult than it looked. On paper, it might be pretty easy to draw some shapes and then draw a line representing the ball's path from start to finish. However, in practice, you have to worry about friction and a spinning ball. Your ball doesn't rebound perfectly off the obstacles—it slows down a bit and its spin can change, changing its direction. If you tried to design a very complex hole that required multiple bounces to get from start to finish in one shot, this might have proved very challenging in real life! With practice, however, you could probably get a hole in one on a hole that only required one or two bounces. Real mini-golf course designers have to take these same principles into account. They don't want the course design to be too easy—holes in one wouldn't be very exciting if they happened all the time. Conversely, they don't want the game to be too difficult and frustrating for players, or it wouldn't be any fun.

CLEANUP

Put away your materials. Be sure not to leave parts of the golf course laying around where others can trip over them.

Measure Earth's Circumference with a Shadow

THE EARTH IS MASSIVE, BUT YOU DON'T NEED A MASSIVE RULER TO MEASURE ITS SIZE. ALL YOU NEED ARE A FEW HOUSEHOLD ITEMS—AND A LITTLE BIT OF GEOMETRY!

If you wanted to measure the circumference of Earth, how long would your tape measure have to be? Would you need to walk the whole way around the world to find the answer? Do you think you can do it with just a yardstick in one location? Try this project to find out! Before you begin, however, it is important to note this project will only work within about two weeks of either the spring or fall equinoxes (usually around March 20 and September 23, respectively).

PROJECT TIME

15 to 20 minutes

KEY CONCEPTS

Mathematics
Geometry
Circumference
Angles
Earth's equator

BACKGROUND

What is Earth's circumference? In the age of modern technology, this may seem like an easy question for scientists to answer with tools such as satellites and GPS—and it would be even easier for you to look up the answer online. It might seem like it would be impossible for you to measure the circumference of our planet using only a yardstick. The Greek mathematician Eratosthenes, however, was able to estimate Earth's circumference more than 2,000 years ago, without the aid of any modern technology. How? He used a little knowledge about geometry!

At the time, Eratosthenes was in the city of Alexandria in Egypt. He read that in a city named Syene south of Alexandria, on a particular day of the year at noon, the sun's reflection was visible at the bottom of a deep well. This meant the sun had to be directly overhead. (Another way to think about this is that perfectly vertical objects would cast no shadow.) On that same day in Alexandria, a vertical object did cast a shadow. Using geometry, he calculated the circumference of Earth based on a few things that he knew (and one he didn't):

- He knew there are 360 degrees in a circle.
- He could measure the angle of the shadow cast by a tall object in Alexandria.
- He knew the overland distance between Alexandria and Syene. (The two cities were close enough that the distance could be measured on foot.)
- The only unknown in the equation was the circumference of Earth!

The resulting equation was:

Angle of shadow in Alexandria / 360 degrees = Distance between Alexandria and Syene / Circumference of Earth

In this project, you will do this calculation yourself by measuring the angle formed by a yardstick's shadow at your location. You will need to do the test near the fall or spring equinoxes, when the sun is directly overhead at Earth's equator. Then you can look up the distance between your city and the equator and use the same equation Eratosthenes used to calculate Earth's circumference. How close do you think your result will be to the "real" value?

There is a geometric rule about the angles formed by a line that intersects two parallel lines. Eratosthenes assumed the sun was far enough away from our planet that its rays were effectively parallel when they arrived at Earth. This told him the angle of the shadow he measured in Alexandria was equal to the angle between Alexandria and Syene, measured at Earth's center. If this sounds confusing, don't worry! It is much easier to visualize with a picture.

MATERIALS

- Sunny day on or near the spring or fall equinoxes (about March 20 or September 23, respectively)
- Flat, level ground that will be in direct sunlight around noon
- Yardstick
- Volunteer to help hold the yardstick while you take measurements. (Or, if you are doing the test alone, you can use a bucket of sand or dirt to insert one end of the yardstick to hold it upright.)
- Stick or rock to mark the location of the shadow
- Calculator
- Protractor
- Long piece of string
- Optional: plumb bob (you can make one by tying a small weight to the end of a string) or post level to make sure the meter stick is vertical

PREPARATION

- Look at your local weather forecast a few days in advance and pick a day where it looks like it will be mostly sunny around noon. (You have a window of several weeks to do this project, so don't get discouraged if it turns out to be cloudy! You can try again).
- Look up the sunrise and sunset times for that day in your local newspaper or on a calendar or a weather or astronomy website. You will need to calculate "solar noon," the time exactly half-way between sunrise and sunset, which is when the sun will be directly overhead. This will probably not be exactly 12 o'clock noon.
- Go outside and set up your materials about 10 minutes before solar noon so you have everything ready.

PROCEDURE

- Set up your meter stick vertically, outside in a sunny spot just before solar noon.
- If you have a volunteer to help, have them hold the yardstick. Otherwise, bury one end of the yardstick in a bucket of sand or dirt so it stays upright.
- If you have a post level or plumb bob, use it to make sure the yardstick is perfectly vertical. Otherwise, do your best to eyeball it.
- At solar noon, mark the end of the yardstick's shadow on the ground with a stick or a rock.
- Draw an imaginary line between the top of the yardstick and the tip of its shadow. Your goal is to measure the angle between this line and the yardstick. Have your volunteer stretch a piece of string between the top of the yardstick and the end of its shadow.
- Use a protractor to measure the angle between the string and the yardstick in degrees. Write this angle down.
- Look up the distance between your city and the equator.
- Calculate the circumference of the Earth using this equation:
  Circumference = 360 x distance between your city and the equator / angle of shadow that you measured
- *What value do you get? How close is your answer to the true circumference of Earth (see "Observations and results" section)?*

SCIENCE FAIR IDEA

Ask a friend or family member in a different city to try the test on the same day and compare your results. *Do you get the same answer?*

SCIENCE FAIR IDEA

Try repeating your test on different days before, on, and after the equinox, or at different times before, at, and after solar noon. *How much does the accuracy of your answer change?*

OBSERVATIONS AND RESULTS

In 200 B.C., Eratosthenes estimated Earth's circumference at about 28,735 miles (46,250 km) Today we know our planet's circumference is roughly 24,850 miles (40,000 km). Not bad for a more than 2,000-year-old estimate made with no modern technology! Depending on the error in your measurements—such as the exact day and time you did the test, how accurately you were able to measure the angle or length of the shadow and how accurately you measured the distance between your city and the equator—you should be able to calculate a value fairly close to the actual number (within a few hundred or maybe a few thousand). All without leaving your own backyard!

CLEANUP

Put away any materials you used.

Human Body Ratios

IF YOU KNOW YOUR HEIGHT, CAN YOU PREDICT HOW BIG YOUR ARM SPAN IS? WHAT ABOUT THE LENGTH OF YOUR FEMUR OR THE CIRCUMFERENCE OF YOUR HEAD? TRY THIS SIMPLE ACTIVITY AND FIND OUT HOW KNOWING THESE SIMPLE RATIOS CAN MAKE YOU A BETTER ARTIST!

PROJECT TIME

20 to 45 minutes

KEY CONCEPTS

Ratios
Mathematics
Biology
Human body

Our bodies are amazing! They are full of mysteries and surprising facts such as this one: Did you know that you are about 0.4 inch (1 cm) taller in the morning, when you have just woken up after hours of lying down, than you are in the evening? You might never have noticed it. These interesting facts only reveal themselves when you look closely, measure, and compare. That is what this activity is about: recording, comparing, and discovering how the human body measures up!

BACKGROUND

Did you know that human bodies come in all sizes and forms? When you start measuring them, however, you will find our bodies show surprising similarities—and even more surprisingly, we can express these with mathematical concepts.

For one thing, our bodies are quite symmetrical. When you draw a vertical line down the center of a body, the left and right sides are almost mirror images of each other. Human bodies also show interesting ratios. Ratios compare two quantities, like the size of one part of the body to the size of another part or to the size of the whole. An example of a human body ratio is a person's arm span—the distance from the middle fingertip of the left hand to that of the right hand when stretching out both arms horizontally—to their height. This ratio is approximately a one-to-one ratio, meaning that a person's arm span is generally about equal to their height. There are many more human body ratios; some are independent of age, and others change as we grow from a baby to an adult.

Wondering who would be interested in these ratios? Artists are avid users of human body ratios because ratios help them draw realistic-looking figures. They are also used in the medical world; a sizable deviation from a human body ratio can indicate a body that is not developing according to expectations. In this science activity, we will examine some human body ratios and, if you like, we can explore how they can help you draw more realistic-looking figures.

MATERIALS

- Yarn
- Scissors
- A hardcover book
- A helper
- Pen and paper (optional)
- Measuring tape (optional)

PREPARATION

- To compare the length of different parts of your body with your height, we will first create a string the length of your height. Take off your shoes. The easiest way is to lie on the ground with your heels pressing against a wall. Look straight up and have your helper place a hardcover book flat against the top of your head, resting on the ground. Get out from under the book and, together, span the yarn across the floor from the wall to the book, cutting the yarn just where it reaches it. Now you have a piece of yarn that is as long as you are tall. (If lying on the ground is not possible, you can also stand flat on the floor against the wall and have the book rest on top of your head and against the wall.)

PROCEDURE

- First, we examine your arm span to height ratio. Your arm span is the distance between the middle fingertips on each hand when you stretch your arms out as far as they can reach. *How do you think your height compares with your arm span? Would it be similar, way longer, or way shorter?*

- Now stretch your arms out as far as they can reach. Your arms will be parallel to the ground. Hold one end of the piece of yarn you just cut off with the fingertips of your left hand. Let your helper span the yarn toward the tip of your right hand's middle finger. *Is the piece of yarn long enough, way longer, or way too short? What does this tell you about how your arm span compares to your height?*

- For most people, their arm span is about equal to their height. Mathematicians say the arm span to height ratio is one to one: your arm span goes once into your height.

- Now let's explore another ratio: the length of your femur bone to your height. The femur bone is the only bone in your thigh. To measure its length, sit down and span a new piece of yarn over your thigh from the hip joint to the edge of your knee and cut the yarn there.

- Make an estimate. *How many times would this piece of yarn go into the piece that is as long as you are tall? Can you find a way to test your estimate?*

- There are several ways to compare the length of the two pieces of yarn: You might cut several pieces of the length of your shorter string, lay them end to end next to your longer piece, and count how many you need. Another way is to fold the longer string into equal parts so the length of the folded string equals the length of the shorter string. The number of folds needed is exactly the number of times your shorter string goes into your longer string.

- *Did you see that the length of your femur bone goes about four times into your height?* You can also say that if you divide your height in four equal pieces, you have the length of your femur bone, or the length of your femur bone is one fourth of your height. Mathematicians call this a one to four ratio.

- Now let's move on to a ratio that might help you make more realistic drawings: the head to body ratio. *How many times would the length of your head fit into your height? Maybe four, six or eight times?* To test six times, fold the yarn with length equaling your height into six equal pieces. Have your helper place a book flat on your head and hang the folded string from the side of the book. If the other end of the string is about level with your chin, your height would be about six times the length of your head, or your head to body ratio would be one to six. *Which number of folds fits best for you?*

- There are many more bodily ratios you can explore: the circumference of your head compared with your height or the length ratios of your forearm and foot or thumb and hand. Use pieces of yarn to measure, compare, and detect these and/or your other bodily ratios.

SCIENCE FAIR IDEA

You have explored some ratios in your body and might wonder if these hold for other people as well. *Do you think they hold for most people of your age? What about adults or babies? Do you think these ratios hold for them or would some be different? Make a hypothesis, find some volunteers, measure, and compare. Was your hypothesis correct?*

SCIENCE FAIR IDEA

This activity uses pieces of yarn to compare lengths. You can also measure your height, arm span, femur bone, etc. with measuring tape, round the values, and write the ratios as fractions. *Can you find a way to simplify these fractions?*

SCIENCE FAIR IDEA

Draw some stick figures on a sheet of paper. *Can you apply some of the bodily ratios you explored (like the arm span to height or the head to body ratio) to the figures? Which ones look most realistic to you?*

SCIENCE FAIR IDEA

Ratios are all around us. *Can you find other places where ratios play an important role?* To get you started, think about a recipe and the ratio of the quantity of one ingredient to another. *For avid bikers, can you find the ratios that correspond to the different gears on a bike?*

OBSERVATIONS AND RESULTS

You probably found your arm span to height ratio approximately to be one to one, whereas the femur to height was approximately one to four. This is expected because on average and over a large age range, the human body has an arm span that is roughly equal to its height and a femur bone roughly a quarter of its height.

The head to body ratio is a little more complex as it changes from a ratio of about one to four for a small child to about one to eight for an adult. A five-year-old is likely to have a head to body ratio of about one to six.

It is good to remember these ratios are averages over a large group of people. Individual variations occur; some might even be used to one's advantage—for example, having exceptionally long arms can be advantageous when playing basketball.

CLEANUP

Put away your materials.

Mesmerizing Fractals

CAN YOU FIND MATH IN ART? IT'S EASY TO SEE IN FRACTALS! YOU CAN MAKE YOUR OWN FRACTAL PRINTS—AND TRACK DOWN THESE FASCINATING SHAPES IN NATURE.

Do you ever wonder what mathematicians study—and why? Most of what they do is complex and difficult to understand, but fractal art might give us a glimpse. Mathematicians study fractals, which are naturally occurring figures used in many branches of science and technology. However, you don't have to be a mathematician to appreciate their beauty. Did you know you can also create one? In this activity, you will get to take out some paint to make artwork—and discover how common fractals are.

PROJECT TIME

60 to 125 minutes

KEY CONCEPTS

Mathematics
Geometry
Fractals
Scale

BACKGROUND

Fractals are geometric figures. They are difficult to define formally, but their features and beauty make them accessible and intriguing.

One feature is self-similarity, which describes how fractals have patterns that recur at different scales. In other words, when you zoom in, you will find a smaller version of a pattern you had seen initially. When you zoom in some more, you will find an even smaller version of that pattern, and so on. This seems to go on infinitely.

The way fractals scale is another feature that sets them apart from traditional geometric figures such as lines, squares, and cubes. When you double the length of a line segment, the original line segment will fit twice in it, making a line one-dimensional. If you double the length of the sides of a square, the original square will fit four times in the new, bigger square, making a square two-dimensional. Do the same on a cube, and the original cube will fit eight times into the new figure, making the cube three-dimensional. Apply this operation on a fractal, and the number of times the original fractal fits into the bigger one could be three or five or any other number that is not a whole power of two. This is characteristic for fractals. They have a fractional dimension, such as 8/5.

A final surprising fact: Some fractals can show an infinite perimeter, even though their area is finite. This is something you can explore in the artwork you are about to create.

MATERIALS

- Old newspaper (to protect your work area)
- Old CD jewel case
- Finger paints
- Paper towels or cloth
- Water
- Paper to make a print (Finger paint paper works best.)
- Magnifying glass (optional)

PREPARATION

- Protect your workspace.
- Disassemble the CD jewel case so you have two loose covers.

- Place one of the covers on your workspace with the flat part facing up, with the edges of the cover below it.

PROCEDURE

- Add a blob of paint about the size of a grape onto the center of the cover.
- Place the second cover on top of the first cover, flat part facing down, so the paint gets squeezed between the flat areas of the two covers and the edges of the covers face out. *What do you notice? Does the paint spread? What type of geometric figure does it form?*
- Look at the perimeter of this figure. *Is it way longer or shorter than the perimeter of the CD cover?*
- *What happens when you lightly press the two covers together and then release again? Does the geometric figure change? Do patterns like cliffs or other branching patterns form?*
- *What do you think will happen when you peel the top cover off? Will the figure change? Will it branch out even more? Will you get two figures, one on each cover? If so, will they be identical?*
- Place the cases back down on your workspace and carefully lift the top cover off. As you do, try not to slide the covers over each other—rather, lift it straight up.
- Look at the resulting figures. *Were your predictions correct?*
- Choose one figure and find a pattern. Then, see if you can find a bigger or smaller version of this pattern in your figure. Mathematicians call figures or patterns that are replicas of each other—but where one can be bigger or smaller than the other—"similar" figures or patterns.

- Place your cover, flat side down, on the paper to form a print. *Do you think the printed figure will be an exact replica of the figure on the CD case? Why or why not?*
- Peel the cover off. Again, avoid sliding the cover over the paper. *Was your prediction correct?* Is your printed version more detailed or less?
- Fractals are geometric figures with patterns that repeat at several levels of magnification. *Can you find smaller and bigger versions of a pattern in your figures?* If you can, you just created fractals!
- If you have a magnifying glass, use it to zoom in and see if you can find the same patterns at an even smaller scale. A pattern that reappears at smaller and smaller scale is a typical feature of a fractal.
- Look at the perimeter of your fractal. Imagine placing fine twine all around your figure, matching the smallest details of its edges and cutting the twine so it can just cover the perimeter of your figure. Then imagine stretching out this piece of twine. *Would it be way longer or shorter than the perimeter of your CD cover?* Now imagine the fractal would branch off into smaller and smaller details. *What would happen to the perimeter of the fractal? Would its area grow as fast? Would this fractal still fit on the CD cover or would it need a bigger surface?*
- Make and study more prints. When you are done printing, clean the covers and repeat the process by adding a new blob of paint. How is your new figure like the first one, and how is it different? Try combining different colors and explore what yields the most beautiful fractals.
- *What do these prints make you think off? Do they resemble something you know?*

SCIENCE FAIR IDEA

Look closely at a broccoli crown or Romanesco broccoli. If you cannot find one in the store, look up some pictures on the internet. *Can you see how the same patterns occur at different sizes?*

SCIENCE FAIR IDEA

Look around you. *Can you find fractals in nature? Look at trees, leaves, ferns, and even clouds. Are these fractals, too? Why or why not?*

SCIENCE FAIR IDEA

Some fractals consist of a figure containing infinitely smaller and smaller versions of itself inside. Look up a Sierpinski triangle online. *Do you see how the pattern infinitely repeats itself at smaller and smaller scale? Can you draw a Sierpinski triangle? Can you make up a fractal of this type yourself?*

SCIENCE FAIR IDEA

Look on the internet for some images of computer-generated fractals and fractals occurring in nature. *Are there some that you find particularly impressive?*

OBSERVATIONS AND RESULTS

Did you find recurring patterns at different scales? Did you see branching patterns occur?

The paint likes to stick together. The interactions within the paint and between the paint and the plastic cover give rise to impressive fractals when you first squeeze the paint between the covers and then release or pull the covers apart. Printing on glossy paper allows you to repeat the process and create patterns that show finer branching.

Although the area of your figure is not changing much, its perimeter grows fast when more and more branching is added.

Fractals are common in nature. Trees, leaves, ferns, shells, lightning, and clouds are just some examples. Fractals are not only around us; they are also inside us: Our lungs and blood vessels show fractal characteristics. Fractal mathematics can help us describe and quantify these structures. Engineers also use fractals to create new products such as cell phone antennas. Fractal art is a form of digital art in which artists use computer-generated images to create intricate objects.

CLEANUP

Wash all equipment with soapy water.

THE SCIENTIFIC METHOD

The scientific method helps scientists—and students—gather facts to prove whether an idea is true. Using this method, scientists come up with ideas and then test those ideas by observing facts and drawing conclusions. You can use the scientific method to develop and test your own ideas!

Question: What do you want to learn? What problem needs to be solved? Be as specific as possible.
Research: Learn more about your topic and refine your question.
Hypothesis: Form an educated guess about what you think will answer your question. This allows you to make a prediction you can test.
Experiment: Create a test to learn if your hypothesis is correct. Limit the number of variables, or elements of the experiment that could change.
Analysis: Record your observations about the progress and results of your experiment. Then analyze your data to understand what it means.
Conclusion: Review all your data. Did the results of the experiment match the prediction? If so, your hypothesis was correct. If not, your hypothesis may need to be changed.

GLOSSARY

abstract: Relating to general ideas or qualities rather than specific people, things, or actions.

beneficial: Producing good results or effects.

biology: A science that deals with living things and their relationships, distribution, and behavior.

calibrate: To make small adjustments for a particular function.

circumference: The perimeter of a circle.

displacement: The action of an object pushing water out of the way to take up that space.

equinox: Either of the two times each year when the sun's center crosses the equator and day and night are everywhere of equal length.

friction: Resistance to motion between bodies in contact.

geometry: A branch of mathematics that deals with points, lines, angles, surfaces, and solids.

innovative: Introducing a new idea, method, or device.

kinetic: Relating to the motions of objects and the forces associated with them.

navigation: The science of figuring out the position and course of a ship or aircraft.

perimeter: The whole outer boundary of a figure or area.

phenomenon: An observable (often rare or important) fact or event.

physics: A science that deals with the facts about matter and motion and includes the subjects of mechanics, heat, light, electricity, sound, and the atomic nucleus.

quantify: To determine, express, or measure how much of something there is.

radius: A straight line extending from the center of a circle to the outside edge or from the center of a sphere to the surface.

sensor: A device that responds to a physical stimulus.

strategy: A carefully developed plan or method for achieving a goal.

theoretical: Something that has not yet been tested or is not able to be fully tested.

ADDITIONAL RESOURCES

Books

Colson, Rob. *Masters of Math.* New York, NY: Crabtree Publishing, 2019.

O'Callaghan, Jonathan, and Simon Basher. *STEM Junior Math.* New York, NY: Kingfisher, 2020.

Shingu, Fumiaki, Corinne Felton, and Erica Williams. *There's Math in My Origami!: 35 Fun Projects for Hands-On Math Learning.* New York, NY: The Experiment, 2021.

Websites

Discovery Education
sciencefaircentral.com

Exploratorium
https://www.exploratorium.edu/search/science%20fair%20projects

Science Buddies
https://www.sciencebuddies.org/science-fair-projects/project-ideas/list

Science Fun
https://www.sciencefun.org/?s=science+fair

Videos

"The Art of Math."
https://ny.pbslearningmedia.org/resource/mgbh.math.rp.artmath/the-art-of-math/. PBS Learning Media, 2:13.

"Math Magic."
https://ny.pbslearningmedia.org/resource/42439c47-de30-487c-9c10-563367a2c843/math-magic/. PBS Learning Media, 1:33.

INDEX